MOSES

God's Chosen Leader

By Anne de Graaf

Illustrated by José Pérez Montero

Moses

God's Chosen Leader

Written by Anne de Graaf
Illustrated by José Pérez Montero
Graphic design by Nils V. Glistrup

Drejervej 15, 3rd floor, DK 2400 Copenhagen NV, Denmark
E-Mail: info@sph.as Web: www.sph.as

Conceived, designed and produced by Scandinavia Publishing House

Printed in China
ISBN 9788771325874

MOSES

God's Chosen Leader

By Anne de Graaf

Illustrated by José Pérez Montero

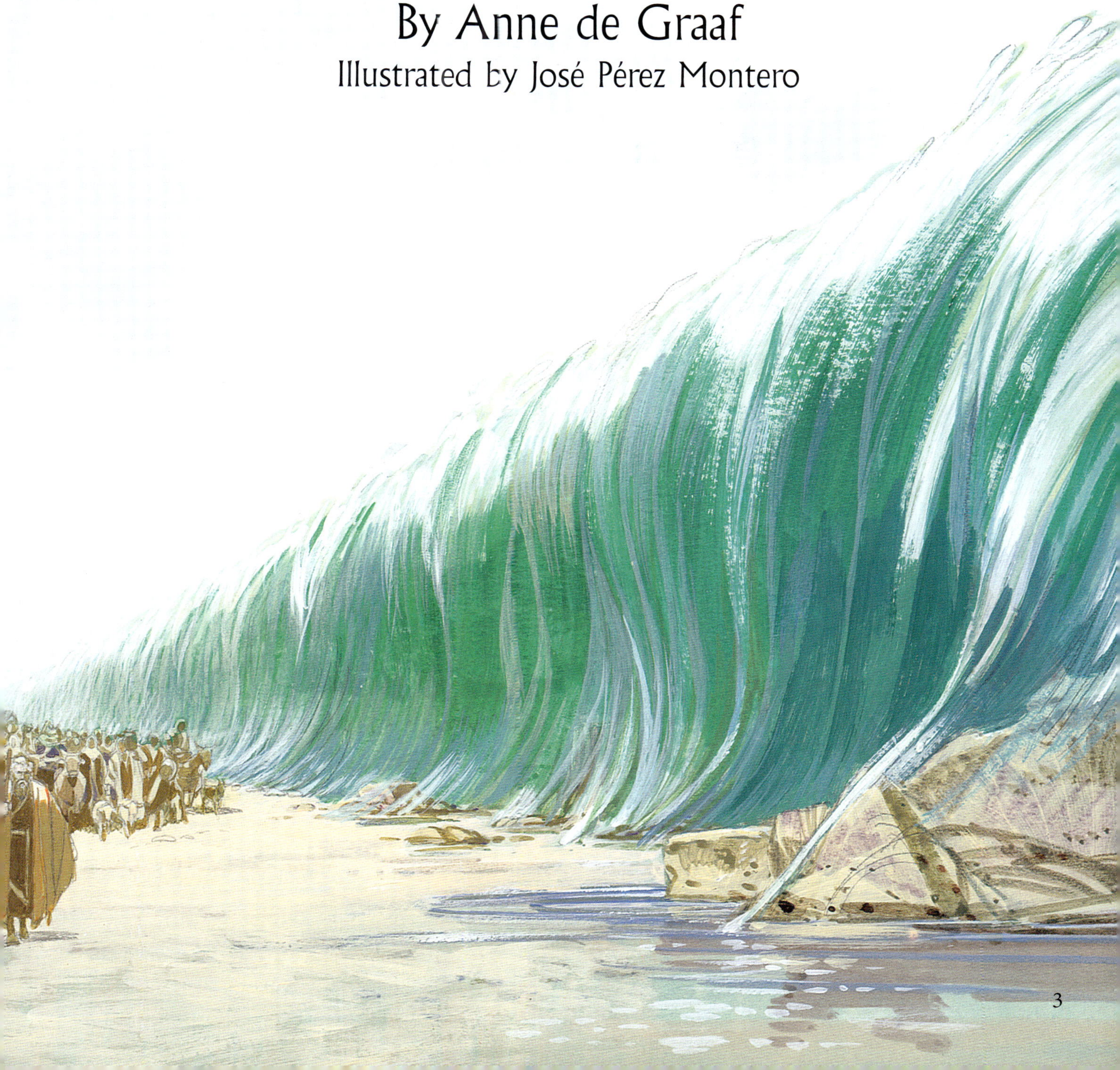

A very, very long time ago, a special little baby boy was born. He lived in Egypt. His family was not Egyptian, though. They were Hebrews, or Israelites.

The Israelites had come to Egypt hundreds of years before this baby was born. At that time the Egyptians had made them welcome. But in the hundreds of years since then, there had been many Israelites born. Now the Egyptians were afraid of the Israelites, so they made them into slaves!

This meant that when this baby was born, his mother had to hide him. The pharaoh, or Egyptian king, had ordered all Israelite boys to be killed! Only the girls could live, and only if they worked as slaves.

All babies are beautiful. This one was extra special. "I just know in my heart, he will grow up to be someone great," his mother told her two older children.

The one brother was named Aaron. He had not been killed by the soldiers. Now the family asked God to protect this second son as well. "Please show us a way to save him," they prayed. They were not afraid of the pharaoh. And then they thought of a plan.

When the pharaoh's soldiers were not looking, the family brought the baby to the great River Nile. They wrapped him in his favorite blanket and placed him into a basket. Then the mother said a prayer, "Lord, please don't let our son drown or be found by the Egyptian soldiers!"

Down the river floated the baby! The quiet lapping of the waves rocked him slowly to sleep.

"A baby! Look everyone! It's a baby in a basket!" The pharaoh's daughter had come to the river for a swim. When she saw the basket floating down the river, though, she had told a servant to bring it to her. Now she looked down at the baby and said, "Oh, poor thing. He must be one of the Hebrew children." She felt sorry for the child. "Look how he's sucking his hand. He's hungry!"

The baby's sister had followed the basket down the river. Now she stepped forward. "Shall I ask one of the Hebrew women to nurse him for you?" She meant her mother, of course.

"Yes, that would be good for him," the princess said. "I will make this boy my own. Tell the soldiers that if they bother you. When he's old enough to eat solid food, bring him to the palace. He will grow up as my son."

His real mother was overjoyed to welcome the child back home. The family thanked God for answering their prayers. Yes, this certainly was a very special baby.

A year or so later his sister brought the baby to the princess. "Oh, look at how cute he is!" The pharaoh's daughter took the baby into her arms. "I will call him Moses. That's a good name, don't you think so?"

Moses' sister smiled. She knew her little brother was in good hands. She went home and together with her parents, prayed for Moses. At least now he would not have to grow up as a slave.

The princess did take good care of Moses. She loved him and gave him the best of everything. As Moses grew older he learned all about the history of Egypt. He also learned about his own group of people, the Hebrews.

"But why are all the Hebrews slaves?" he asked his mother.

"Because the pharaoh needs workers. He needs people to take care of the fields and build the pyramids."

"But it's not fair!" young Moses cried. "I've seen the Egyptians whip my people. Sometimes they don't even have enough to eat!"

His adopted mother looked away. "Yes, I know, Moses. But there's nothing we can do about it. Remember why you are a prince. My father, your grandfather, is the mighty pharaoh. We must all do as he says."

Moses thought, "I will do something! It's not right. My history teachers told me the Hebrews came here to work with the Egyptians, not for them!"

Years went by and in that time Moses also learned there was a difference between the Egyptian gods, which were not real, and the God of the Hebrews, who is very real.

When Moses was about forty years old he finally had a chance to do something for his people. One day, he was walking home to the palace when he turned a corner and saw an Egyptian beating up a Hebrew slave!

Moses could not hold himself back. "You there!" he ran toward the man. "This is the last time you ever hit one of my people!" The Egyptian looked up in surprise. Moses hit him as hard as he could. Over and over they tumbled in the sand. Then Moses killed the Egyptian. As fast as he could, Moses buried the body so no one would find it.

The next day Moses saw two slaves fighting. "Stop this!" he pulled them apart. "You should be fighting the Egyptians, not each other."

"Who do you think you are?" They turned on Moses. "We saw you kill that Egyptian yesterday!"

Moses gasped, "You know!"

"Who doesn't?" The two slaves laughed at Moses.

Moses ran for his life.

Moses left Egypt and his life as a prince far behind. Moses ran deep, deep into the desert. The pharaoh's guards came back empty-handed. Moses had disappeared without a trace. Or had he?

Once Moses knew he was safe, he asked himself, "I've run away, but now what do I do? I don't know how to find food in the desert. What if I die?" A few days later Moses found a well.

There he saw several shepherds who would not let some women get their water.

Moses chased away the bullies. When he helped the women, they invited him home for a meal.

The women were sisters. Their father was a wise man belonging to a tribe which traveled through the desert. They lived in tents and kept sheep. Moses became a good friend of the father. He married one of the daughters and spent the next forty years working as a shepherd.

During that time Moses learned that he was not the important prince he once had been in Egypt. Out in the desert he was just an ordinary shepherd.

More than once under those huge night skies, Moses mumbled to himself, "There's nothing special about me. All I'm good at is running away." Moses did not like himself very much. Then something happened that changed his life forever.

One day, Moses was at the foot of a mountain, looking for some sheep. They had wandered off among the rocks and high cliffs.

All at once he saw something very strange.

"A fire!" He waited to see which way the fire would spread. Would the wind blow it toward Moses and his flock or away from them? It did neither. The fire stayed in one spot!

Moses could not believe his eyes. He walked closer and a shiver ran up his back. "What's this?" he asked out loud.

The bush was on fire, but did not burn! Inside the fire the bush was still green.

Suddenly, Moses heard a voice speak out of the flames. "Moses, Moses!"

"Here I am."

The voice coming from the bush said, "I am the God of your fathers, the God of Abraham, Isaac, and Jacob, the God of the Israelites."

As Moses knelt, God said, "I have seen the Egyptians hurt My people all these years. I have heard them crying out for help. I know their pain. Now the time has come for you to lead them out of Egypt. Take them into the land I promised My people so long ago. Speak to Pharaoh. Tell him to let My people go."

Moses shook his head. "But I'm nobody," he thought to himself. "I'm only good at running away. Why does God choose a loser like me?"

Out loud, Moses said, "But. . .but why should I be the one to speak to Pharaoh?"

"Because I will be with you. You're My chosen leader."

Moses shuddered. "But. . .I can't! What would I tell them? Who do I say sent me?"

"Tell them the Lord God has sent you," God answered.

Moses felt miserable. "I'm no good," he thought to himself. So he argued with God. He did not want the job. "But. . . but why should they believe me? What sign can I give them that I've been sent by God?"

"When you throw your staff to the ground it will become a snake. When you pick it up again it will become a staff. Try it."

Moses threw his staff on the ground. When it wiggled away as a snake, Moses cried out and ran away. Then Moses stepped over to the snake and picked it up. In his hands it became a wooden staff again.

Moses was afraid. "But. . .but I. . .don't speak well. How am I going to tell the pharaoh that he should set the Hebrews free? He won't listen to me! Please. . ."

The Lord said to him, "Just go and I will be with you. I will teach you what to say."

Moses' fear made him foolish. "Please, please send someone else."

The flames from the bush grew brighter and more fierce. "What about your brother Aaron?" God said. This was the older brother who had prayed with Moses' family when Moses was just a tiny baby.

God said, "He can speak well. I will send him here to meet you. All you have to do is tell him what to say and he will help you. I have chosen you to lead the people, though. Now go!"

Moses hung his head. What more could he say? Moses finally accepted what God had asked of him. Only then did God take care of Moses' fear. He told him, "The pharaoh and his men who were trying to kill you are all dead now. There is another pharaoh. He will not hurt you."

Moses nodded. He felt as if he were taking a big step down a long, dark tunnel. Moses heard in his thoughts God's promise, "I will be with you."

On the way to Egypt, Moses did meet his brother Aaron. Moses told him everything that had happened. The brothers traveled the rest of the way together. They were on a mission from God.

"But you must believe us!" Aaron spoke to the Hebrew leaders in Egypt. Every one of the old men at the meeting were slaves. Some were shaking their heads at what Aaron said, "God has chosen Moses to lead you out of Egypt."

Moses stepped forward. He took a deep breath and said, "Watch this. This is the sign we will show Pharaoh so he will let you go!" Moses threw his staff on the floor.

When the staff turned into a snake, everyone gasped, "Yes, they really are from God!"

"We believe! Tell us what to do!"

Aaron said, "Pray for us. Now we give Pharaoh God's message."

As they approached Pharaoh's palace, Moses felt like running away again. He looked at his brother walking next to him. Then Moses looked up at the gates. "This is it," he mumbled. Moses knew what he had to do.

Once inside the palace, Moses walked down the same halls he had played in as a boy.

"What do you want?" the great and mighty pharaoh of Egypt growled.

"We have a message from the great and mighty God of our fathers. He says you should let all the Hebrew slaves leave Egypt."

Pharaoh laughed. "Ha! A god of slaves! What nonsense! Get out of my sight!"

Moses and Aaron looked at each other. This was not going to be easy. "The God of the Hebrews says He wants His people to leave Egypt for three days and worship Him."

"Don't be ridiculous!" Pharaoh roared. "Slaves can't take a vacation! It's just because you are lazy! The Hebrews work for me and no one else!'

Moses and Aaron had warned the pharaoh. He had chosen not to listen. Even when he saw the staff turn into a snake, Pharaoh said, "That's just a wizard's trick! Look!" At that the king's wizards did the same thing with their staffs. They turned into snakes too! But Moses' staff swallowed them up!

Still, Pharaoh did not believe in God. Now God would give Pharaoh ten very good reasons why he should let His people go. God told Moses, "I will send ten plagues to Egypt. After the plagues, all Egyptians, even Pharaoh, will know I am God. Then he will let My people go."

The ten plagues were horrible! First God changed all the water in Egypt into blood. All the fish died. Pharaoh could not take a bath!

Then God sent thousands of frogs. Moses had warned Pharaoh, "God says to let His people go." Pharaoh had not listened. The frogs hopped their way out of the rivers and ponds and into the Egyptians' homes. That's when Pharaoh called Moses.

"Get rid of them! Do whatever you have to, but stop these frogs!"

"God says, 'Let My people go.'"

"All right! Yes, tomorrow. They can all leave tomorrow, anything, just get rid of the frogs. They're all over the kitchens and I even found one in my bed!"

When all the frogs had gone, though, Pharaoh changed his mind. "No! The slaves may not go free. I need them to work!"

So God sent swarms of tiny and big flies. They landed on everything. All the animals and people were covered with the creeping, crawling flies. The tiny flies were the worst.

Then God sent a sickness so that all the Egyptians' cattle died. During these last plagues only the Egyptians and their homes were harmed. God was careful to spare the Hebrews and their animals.

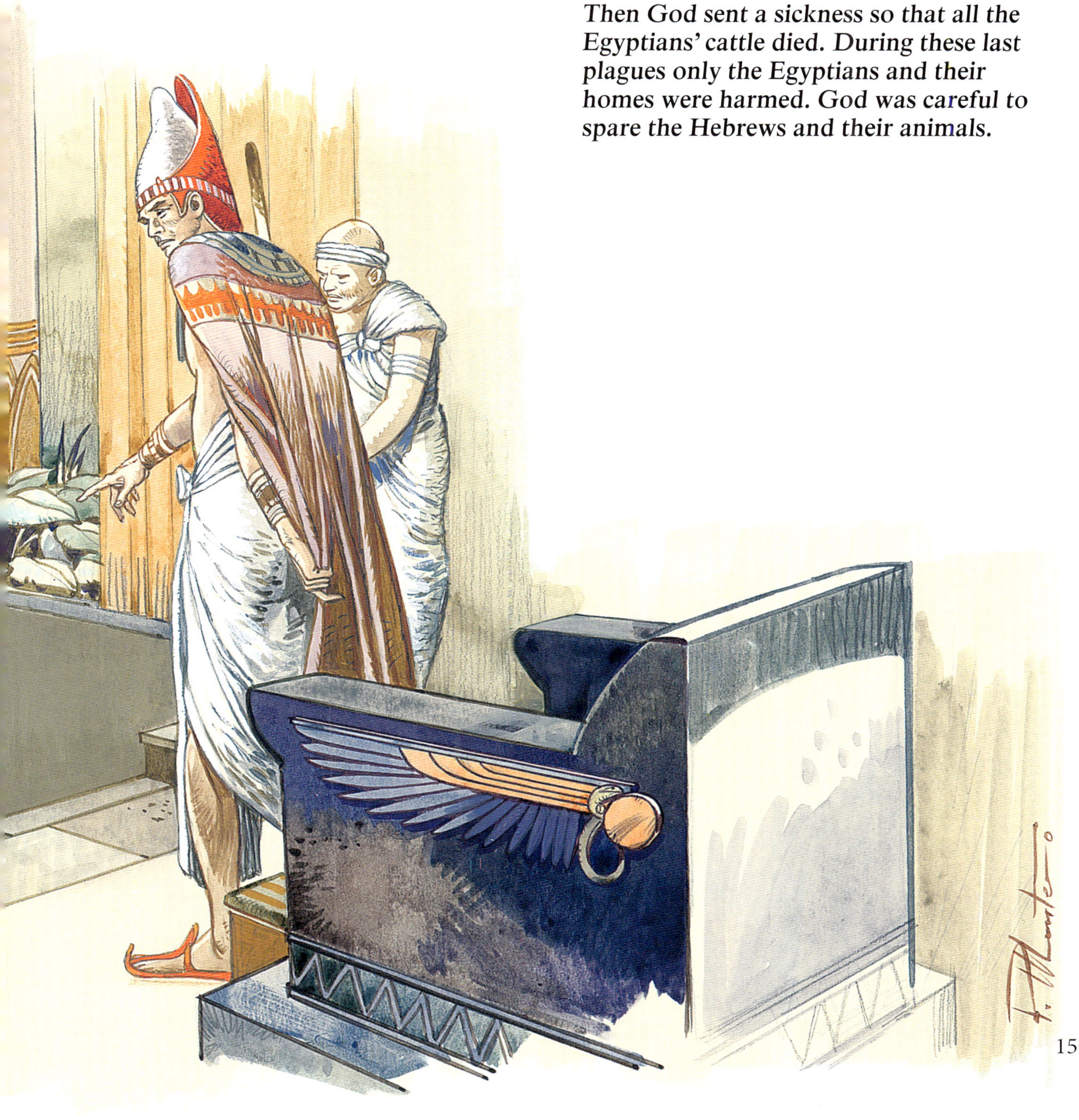

Every time a new plague hit Egypt, Pharaoh sent for Moses. "Make it stop and I'll let the Hebrews go free," he begged. Each time, Moses went to the Lord in prayer and God stopped the plague. But then Pharaoh would change his mind, again and again.

God sent a fine dust to fall from the sky. It landed on all the Egyptians' faces, then grew into horrible sores! "Agh! What is wrong with us?" the Egyptians cried.

The Israelites shook their heads. There was nothing wrong with their skin. "You should tell your pharaoh to let us go."

The Egyptians pleaded with Pharaoh. Even his own magicians and servants begged him to let the Hebrews go free. "Their God is too strong for us," they said.

Pharaoh shook his head. "They aren't going anywhere but back to work, where they belong!" he boomed.

Then the Lord sent the worst hailstorm Egypt had ever seen. Thunder shook the land as fire and hail fell from the sky. Anyone caught outside was killed by the huge hailstones. They were as big as melons! All the plants and grass were crushed flat.

Then God sent a huge cloud of locusts, which ate every green leaf in Egypt. They covered all the ground until it was black. But where the Israelites were living it was light. Pharaoh finally said, "Enough! Take your people and leave us alone!" But then he changed his mind again!

God sent darkness to settle over the land. Day became night and night lasted for days. Again Pharaoh told Moses, "Leave

us. Go now! But make sure you leave your sheep and cattle behind." He was very angry and once again, Pharaoh changed his mind He still would not let God's people go.

Finally, the Lord said to Moses, "I will bring one more plague on Egypt. After that Pharaoh will let you go. But first you must protect yourselves against what I am about to do."

Moses had learned a great deal while all this was happening. He had learned that God means what He says. Now Moses warned God's people that they should paint their doors with lamb's blood. That night God would cause every eldest son to die in his bed. This would happen in most of the Egyptian homes, but not in the homes of the Hebrews. The lamb's blood would protect the Israelites. In the years to come, God's people would always remember that night as the very first Passover.

God's people were ready to leave Egypt. They stood eating their last meal. In all the Hebrew homes, people wore cloaks and sandals, travel clothes. They were going on a long journey to a new land, free at last! And God's promise to Abraham was finally coming true. It was a new beginning and they were filled with hope.

"What will it be like?"

"How far will we have to walk?" All night long the Israelites asked Moses questions.

Moses looked around "How has it happened?" he asked himself. "I always thought I was a coward, and now I'm leading all these people away from the great and mighty pharaoh." All the hundreds and thousands of people had packed their things and were waiting for Moses to give the word. Would Pharaoh finally let them go?

Halfway through the night, Moses and his people heard a strange sound. Everyone stopped talking and listened. Crying. They heard the sounds of people weeping.

"It's time!" Moses told them. The word spread. A knock on the door, the shout, that was the signal. It was time to go! Pharaoh had finally given the word. They were free!

The Israelites dashed outside. Then they knew, the crying was coming from the Egyptian homes. They had all lost their eldest sons. Even Pharaoh had found his son dead. And now a terrible grief shook the land.

But the Israelites had been spared because they had done what God told them to do during Passover. They were God's people. If Pharaoh had believed in God, his people would have been spared too. But he chose not to believe. Now Pharaoh's heart was broken.

"Tell them to leave! Out of Egypt! I want those Hebrews gone and out of my sight!" Pharaoh sobbed.

The Israelites left Egypt as fast as they could. They took their sheep and cattle, some clothes, and a little food. Moses led the way. During the day he followed a tall, thin cloud. At night the cloud became a pillar of fire, reaching down from heaven. This was God's way of guiding Moses and the people.

Day and night, night and day, Moses led God's people through the desert. They were afraid Pharaoh might change his mind.

One evening the Israelites thought they could feel the pounding of hoofbeats in the sand. "We're imagining things!" They laughed at each other. They had just arrived at the sea and were setting up camp.

A little boy knelt down. He put his ear to the sand. "It's thumping!" The whole camp looked back the way they had just come.

Their hearts stopped.

"Pharaoh! He's coming after us!"

"Look at his army! The chariots!"

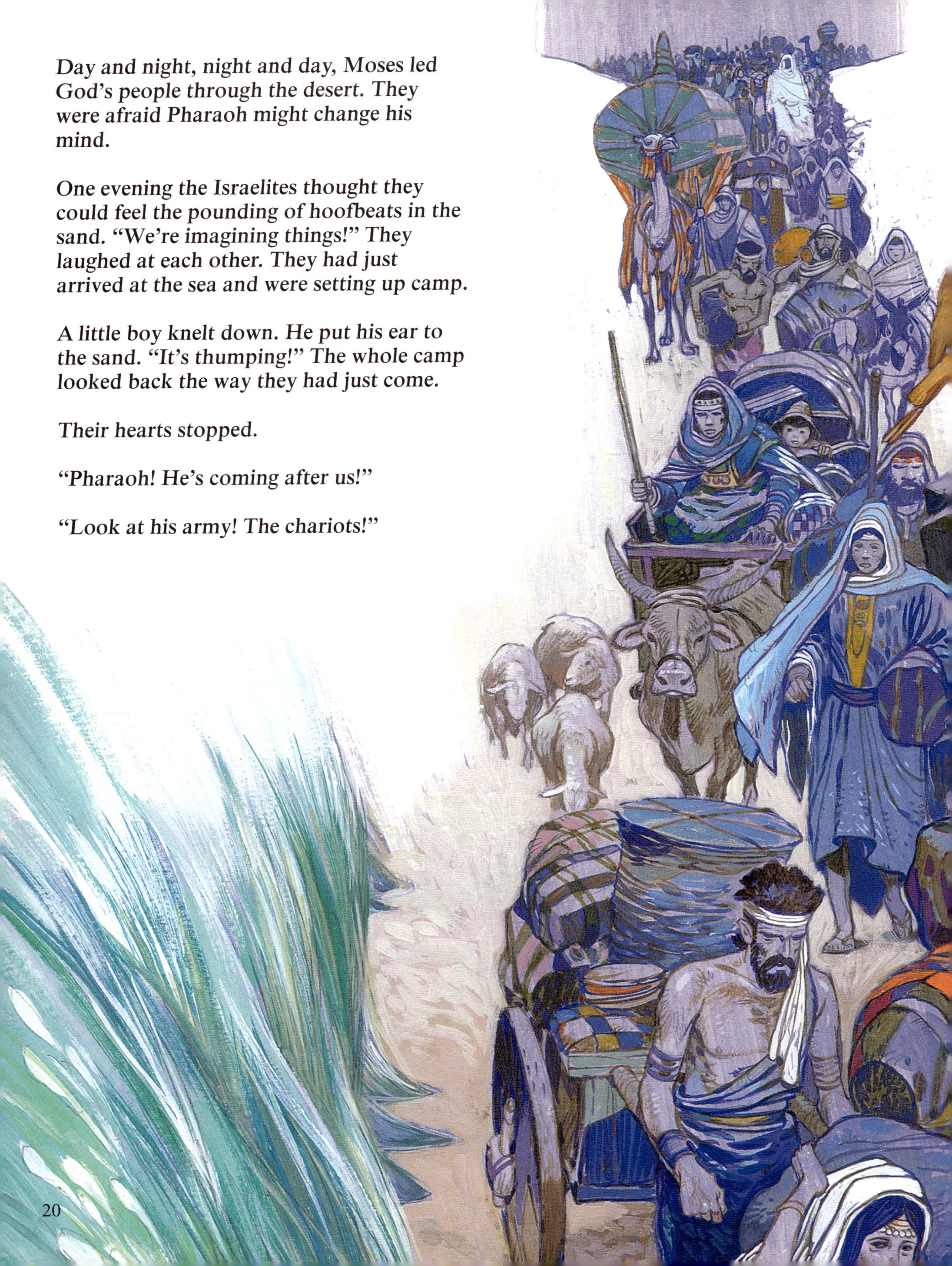

"Oh, we should have stayed in Egypt!"

"Where can we go? We're trapped by the sea!"

Moses did not have time to feel scared. He tried to calm the people, but they started running around and screaming. He said, "God, has told me He will fight for you. He says this is the last time you will ever see these Egyptians."

Then Moses stretched out his staff over the sea. The people heard a great roar as the sea split in two! Straight down the middle of the sea rose a dry path.

"Go!" Moses ordered the people. "You're not trapped anymore. God has shown us

a way out. Now hurry!"
All night long the Israelites crossed the sea. Every single one arrived safely on the other side. All their sheep and cattle made it across, as well.

In the morning, the Egyptians reached the water, just as the last Israelite scrambled up onto the other side. "If they can cross the sea, so can we!" Pharaoh ordered. The chariots plunged onto the dry path through the sea.

The Israelites looked at Moses. "Now what do we do?"

Just as all the Egyptians were between the waves, Moses reached out toward the sea again. Another terrible roar shook the ground!

Moses stretched his staff over the water. The waves on both sides of the Egyptian army crashed down on top of them! God swept them away, covering them with water! Pharaoh and his men disappeared into the depths!

The people had never seen anything like it before. They cheered Moses. They cheered God. "There is no God like ours! Oh let's thank Him for saving us!" they cried. It was their first party as a free people. How they celebrated!
Moses clapped his hands and danced with the others. "Lord," he prayed, "You were right. You did stay by my side. I did not think I could lead the people and escape Egypt. But You made it happen. Thank You!" More than anything else, Moses hoped that the Israelites would never forget how much God had shown His love for them.

Now all the years Moses had spent in the desert proved useful. He knew how to find food and water in the desert. He knew how to sleep during the hot days and travel

during the cool nights.
The people did not, though. And they did not like learning how. Soon after they left the sea, the people started grumbling about the heat, the food, the dryness. "We were better off as slaves in Egypt!" they shouted at Moses.

Moses was their leader. He knew God loved them. "Trust God, hasn't He always taken care of us? He's promised to take us to a new land, a better land. . ." Moses knew God had not left them to die in the desert.
But no one wanted to listen. God made manna, or flakes of light bread to fall from the sky. This way the people would not go hungry. Every morning God rained down manna so the children could help their parents gather it into baskets. The people still grumbled.

Moses finally told the people they could rest and make camp. The place was at the bottom of a mountain called Sinai. God had told Moses to climb the mountain. He had a special gift for Moses and the Israelite people.

Moses was away from the people forty days. All that time he talked with God on the mountaintop. Moses had changed. He did not argue with God anymore. After all he had seen, Moses knew the Lord was very mighty and powerful.

The special gift which God gave Moses was two stone tablets. God had written on these rocks with His own finger. He had written rules which would help His people know the difference between right and

wrong. These were the Ten Commandments. The Ten Commandments were the most important gift God had ever given His people. Moses held the slabs of rock in his hands. He shook with excitement.

But then suddenly God said, "Go down at once! Your people have made a golden calf for themselves. They are calling it god. They say the calf brought them out of Egypt. Go! I will let My anger burn against them and they will be destroyed!" Smoke poured off the mountain.

Moses begged the Lord not to punish the people. "They are like children, Lord. Did You bring them out of Egypt just to have them killed in the desert?"

All this time, Moses was swallowed up in a fire on top of the mountain. This fire was just like the one in the burning bush. Its flames did not burn.
Now it was Moses who stood in the middle of the fire. He was with God, as God had been with him. Moses could feel the heat of God's anger. He waited for an answer.

Finally the Lord said yes to Moses. He would give the Israelites another chance. God had mercy on His people.

Moses thanked God. Then he stepped out of the fire. He was the leader of the people. He would have to teach them what they had done wrong. Moses hurried down the mountain. He carried the tablets of stone carefully all the way to the camp. When he saw the people dancing around their golden calf, though, he stopped, too shocked to

move.
Moses could not believe that the people could be so. . . so blind. Didn't they remember what God had done to the Egyptians? Hadn't they eaten the food He gave them in the desert? Moses looked at the Ten Commandments in his hands. The very first rule told the people not to make any statues or other things and treat them like gods. Moses groaned, "They have already broken the first rule before they

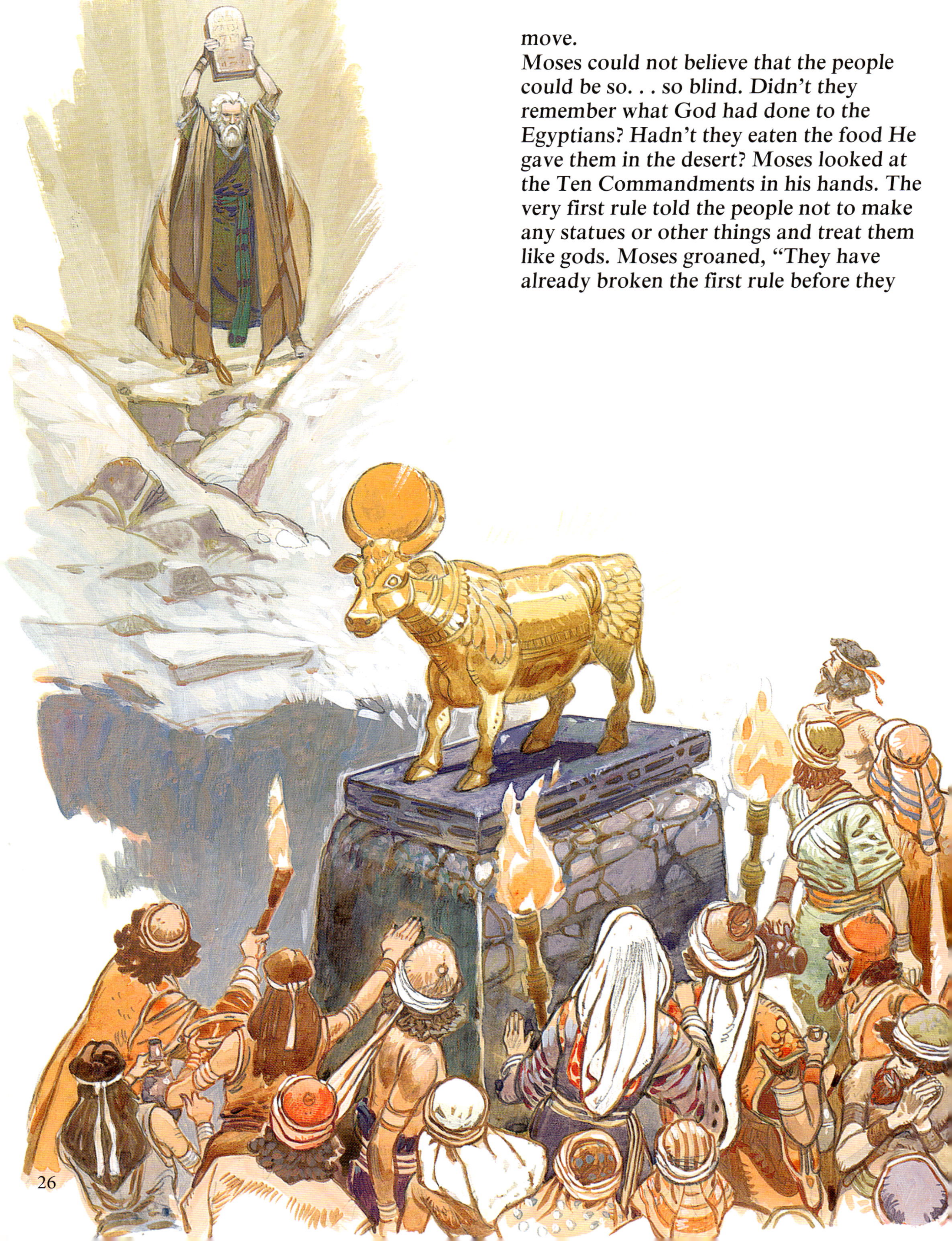

even had a chance to hear it."
Moses was furious! He roared, "Stop! You have done the very worst thing you could have done! You have turned away from God! And for what? A calf of gold!"

With that, Moses raised the tablets over his head and hurled them to the ground. They shattered into a hundred pieces! The rocks, covered with God's own writing, lay broken at the foot of the mountain.

Moses punished the people. The next day he said, "I'm going back up the mountain now. I must talk to the Lord. You have done a terrible thing!"

When Moses was with God again, he said, "Please forgive them, Lord." Moses stayed another forty days on top of Mount Sinai. When the time was up, God told Moses he would let the people start over. He was very disappointed in them, though. The Lord gave Moses another set of stone tablets.

Moses brought these down to the people and read the rules to them. The people promised to try and be good. They listened to the rules and nodded their heads. "Yes," some said. "They make good sense."

Then the people moved on through the desert. They followed wherever Moses led them. No matter how far they went, though, they would never forget the look on Moses' face when he came down from that mountain.

His face had shone like the sun! Moses' face had shone because, during his second time on the mountaintop, Moses saw God. He was the only man to see God face to face. The Lord walked right by Moses. He stood with him, just as any man would stand with his friend. Moses became God's friend. Seeing God had lit up Moses' face!

This was not the only time Moses' face shone from the glory of God. Wherever Moses told the people to camp, he always put up one special tent for the Lord. In that tent Aaron and his sons carefully placed the Ten Commandments.

Moses visited the tent often. He went there to talk with God. He always came out of the tent with his face glowing. This was a sign to the people that their Moses was not just any leader. Moses was God's chosen leader.

Even though the people had promised to be good, it did not take them long to start grumbling and complaining again.

"It's too hot!"

"We should never have left Egypt!" When they did not have enough to eat, they moaned.

"Where is God anyway?" They were not at all thankful for the food and water God gave them every day.

Moses tried his best to teach the people. That is what leaders are for. "Just think of where we are going. God promised to take us safely to a new land, the promised land! Trust Him, He has never forgotten you!" But the people chose not to listen. Even when they had camped at a place very near to the promised land, the people grumbled. "We've seen that land. It's full of enemy tribes!"

"We don't want to live there!" The people shouted at Moses.

"You know what we think? There is no God!" They had completely forgotten the power of God. They had forgotten that they had ever been slaves in Egypt. They had forgotten about Mount Sinai. They stopped following Moses and listening to him. Now there was no way God could reach them with His love.

There was nothing Moses could do. No one would listen to him! Finally God grew so angry at the people that He said they would have to spend forty years wandering through the desert until they arrived at their new homes.

Wandering for forty years meant that all the people who had grumbled would die of old age before they reached the prom-

ised land.
The Lord would start over with the children of those He had brought out of Egypt, the children of the grumblers. In forty years those children would be grown. By then God's people would finally be ready to trust Him.

Moses groaned inside when he heard the news. He had never wanted the job of leading such a stubborn people. Yet now he had forty more years to go before he

finished the job.
During that time he would often sigh, "I don't know if I can do this." Moses felt weak when the people kept making the same mistakes over and over again. He often thought about giving up and saying, "It's no use."

Each time Moses came to God's tent and prayed about his doubts, God said, "Moses, I am with you. I have chosen you." This helped lift Moses' worries. It was enough for Moses that God was on his side.

For forty long years Moses led God's people around, through, in, and out of the desert. A trip which was only about one hundred miles should have only lasted a few weeks. Instead it dragged on for forty years! Throughout it all, there was never one day when Moses stopped trying to be the best leader possible. He was not bossy, but caring, like a shepherd for his sheep.

At the end of that time, all the people who had said they didn't believe in God were dead of old age. Their children were grown and had children of their own. These people believed in God, even though they had not seen what God had done for them in Egypt. They trusted Him and looked forward to seeing the promised land.

One day, God told Moses to hand the job of leader over to someone else. Moses was a hundred and twenty years old. He was the only old person left. Even Aaron was

dead by then.
He called all the people together. "Remember to follow the Law. Listen to your new leader. And never make the same mistakes your parents made. Believe in God and He will always be by your side."

Moses knew what he was talking about. He had started out being the most unsure of men. No matter what, God had always shown him what to do and made everything come out all right. Moses did not take the credit, he gave it all to God.

The time had come for Moses to leave the earth and be with the Lord. All alone he climbed to the top of a mountain. There stretched out before him was the promised land. "I can see it all!" Moses cried. He had led the people so long and so far. This was what he had waited all his life to see.

God had said Moses could look at the land, but he would never actually enter the land. This time Moses did not argue with God. He said yes. After all, Moses was the friend of God. And that made everything worth it.

While standing on that mountain, Moses died. God came and buried Moses' body Himself. Moses was one of the most important men to ever mold the history of God's people. For forty years Moses was a prince. For forty years he thought of himself as a nobody. And for forty years Moses was God's choice to lead His people to the promised land.

You can find the story of Moses in the Old Testament
in the book of Exodus, Numbers, and Deuteronomy.